IDEA TO PROFITABLE CREATIONS WORKBOOK

16 Step Guide to move your ideas from your brain and turn them into real and bankable products, innovations, inventions or creations.

IREDAFENEVESHO OWOLABI

IREDAFENEVESHO OWOLABI

Some other Fast-selling Books By the author are:

- Kingdom Verities
- How to Enjoy Kingdom Currency (Vol. 1)
- How to Maximize Kingdom Currency (Vol. 2)
- Kingdom Currency for Students, Graduates and Businessmen (Vol. 3)
- Unlocking Your Kingdom Creativity
- 4-D THINKING
- Why you should Write a Book
- How to Turn your Knowledge to Money
- How to Turn Wisdom Currency to Money
- How to Make Millions as an Author-preneur
- 18 Steps to Write a Book Successfully
- How to Launch, Sell and Market your Books Profitably
- How to Successfully Self-Publish Your Books
- Hot Markets Where You Can Easily Sell Your Books
- Creativity Accelerator

All books are available for bulk purchase, please contact us via Tel: (+234) 8187960599.

Or

Visit *www.iredafeowolabi.net/shop* for eBooks, Audiobooks, Video and Online programs by the author.

To Contact the author for feedbacks, to share or tell a story perhaps for inclusion in one of the future books by the author or to schedule him for a presentation, kindly send a mail to *info@iredafeowolabi.net* ***or*** *iredafeowolabi@gmail.com*.

TABLE OF CONTENT

IREDAFENEVESHO OWOLABI

INTRODUCTION

Are you struggling with turning those ideas and potentials of yours into profitable creations, innovations, productions and inventions?

Are you willing to create a good side income that fetches you not just more money but extra satisfaction with things that come naturally to you?

Do you want to create a business that works for you rather than the other way round?

If yes, then jump on this guide!

I have prepared it in a manner that would help you engage in some deep-thinking, brainstorming and mindstorming.

If you take it seriously, the results would astound you.

For better results, I advise that you take time to go through all the sections. Any part you cannot give answers to, do some more research and consult some other of my Creativity and 4-D Thinking books in order to make the most of this guidebook. So, grab a pen and get to work as you birth your brainchild.

SECTION I

YOUR INTENTION

- **Your intention is your foremost or major the reason behind the idea to profitable creation process which you are going through or are about to go through.**

1. What idea, creation, production, innovation or invention do you intend to be known for and remembered for? What is that special stuff you are made of?

| |
| |
| |
| |

IREDAFENEVESHO OWOLABI

2. Why do you want to birth these ideas?

3. How do you intend to use your production, creation or innovation to serve others?

IREDAFENEVESHO OWOLABI

4. What do you think is your life's purpose or God's intent for your life and for that brainchild of yours?

5. Why do you think your idea(s) is/are worth producing into tangible results?

SECTION II

IREDAFENEVESHO OWOLABI

YOUR NICHE

- **This is that particular segment or narrow section of the people who should benefit from your brainchild.**

1. Who are your potential customers or beneficiaries of this wonderful brainchild, idea, creation or production of yours?

2. Where are your ideas best-suited to blossom (environment, atmosphere, city, state, country, etc)?

3. Define and describe your ideal customer with gender, age range, religion, culture, habit, education, spending pattern, likes and dislikes, etc.

IREDAFENEVESHO OWOLABI

SECTION III

IREDAFENEVESHO OWOLABI

YOUR DESIGNS

- **This represents the master plan, grand plan and ultimate long-term goal and vision for the birthing of this creation.**

1. What is this burning idea, passion, or desire that you have and what does it look like? Describe it as though you are painting a picture for a blind man to see, then draw a sketch in the diagram box (be vivid and graphic!).

<table>
<tr><td> </td></tr>
<tr><td> </td></tr>
<tr><td> </td></tr>
<tr><td> </td></tr>
<tr><td> </td></tr>
<tr><td> </td></tr>
</table>

IREDAFENEVESHO OWOLABI

SKETCH DIAGRAM

2. What is the concept all about? Have you mapped out what it is supposed to be like when it begins to take shape (babyhood stage of brainchild (idea) development)?

SKETCH DIAGRAM

3. What is the idea supposed to look like when it has been designed, mapped out or planned out? What is it supposed to look like at maturity stage of brainchild (idea) development?

SKETCH

IREDAFENEVESHO OWOLABI

SECTION IV

EXECUTE

- **Creativity is incomplete without execution. For every idea to fulfill its highest purpose, it must be produced into visible, tangible quantities. Without execution, your wonderful ideas would evaporate into thin air without any results to show.**

1. What can you do now in order to start producing your ideas and birthing your brainchild?

2. What are the limitations or hindrances holding you back at the moment?

IREDAFENEVESHO OWOLABI

3. Is capital (money) a hindrance?

_____

_____

_____

4. If yes, is there an intangible value you can offer or serve voluntarily to others in order to create awareness or attention? Remember value attracts money. What free value can you give? Capital is not money, Capital is wisdom! Who can you work for to raise the money? Where can you display or showcase your idea or skill? Go wide with our thoughts!

5. Do you need any specialized training, guide, apprenticeship or coaching before you begin or as you begin?

_____

_____

_____

6. What do you intend to learn through either of these capacity development plans?

7. Who or where do you plan to go to and for how long are you willing to undergo the process?

8. How would you measure the results of the training or development exercise? A certificate or a hands-on skill or know how (remember certificates do not make success, skill and know how-does)?

SECTION V

AUTHENTICATE

- **This means to make your production unique and original like none else that existed before it.**

1. Are there other people in your industry that have done something similar to what the ideas you are trying to produce?

_____

_____

_____

_____

_____

_____

_____

_____

2. Are you copying them or imitating them?

_____

_____

_____

_____

_____

3. If yes, why can't you do otherwise?

IREDAFENEVESHO OWOLABI

4. Instead of copying them, you can learn from them and gain inspiration to birth your own brainchild. Is it possible to reengineer your service, product or creation in a way that makes you authentic and different from the pack? How do you intend to do these? What are the unique things that attract you to them that can be learned? How can you improve on their own model?

| |
| |
| |
| |

5. Who is/are the best in your industry right now?

What makes them authentic, real and original?

6. Picture your idea and creation gaining the number one spot in your industry, what authentic value do you want to be known for that no one else brings to the table?

SECTION VI

IREDAFENEVESHO OWOLABI

SIMPLIFY

The world is already complicated and full of complex problems. People are looking for ways to make their lives easier.

1. What is your commitment to provide your solutions faster and easier?

2. What other solutions do you have for people with different tastes and preferences? (e.g. If you are an author, what other formats can you put your books to make it easier for people to benefit from those creations? If you run a commercial business, what other payment gateways or payment plans are available apart from cash payment? Etc. Please adapt these examples to your peculiar situation!)

IREDAFENEVESHO OWOLABI

SECTION VII

IREDAFENEVESHO OWOLABI

TESTRUN

- **Now you believe so much in this idea of yours that is being turned into a production or creation. You need to do some test run to test the durability of your solutions. For example, many companies in different parts of the world have come up with enticing offers that were not sustainable and have run into a lot of troubles as a result.**

1. Have you tested to see the efficiency of the idea or to see if it actually works?

_____

_____

_____

_____

_____

2. If it is not working properly what do you intend to do? Give up or redesign?

_____

_____

_____

_____

_____

_____

_____

_____

_____

_____

_____

3. What gives you the assurance that it would meet the need or solve the problem you have designed or envisaged it to solve?

IREDAFENEVESHO OWOLABI

SECTION VIII

IREDAFENEVESHO OWOLABI

ORGANIZE

- **In this part, you would identify all your skills, talents, resources, personnel and find a way to organize them all into a system that works in a creative and harmonious order. Some call it "packaging".**

1. What are your strengths?

_____

_____

_____

_____

_____

_____

2. How can these strengths help you realize your goals of birthing your brainchild/idea?

3. Is there a better way to organize these strengths, skills, gifts, potentials, personnel and resources in a way that would produce greater output? If yes, state and expatiate on the way(s) below.

SECTION IX

YOUR COLLABORATIONS

This refers to the team you are going to work with in a complementary environment to ensure that your ideas are effectively produced into the design you had in mine.

1. List the people you desire to collaborate with and why. (What are they bringing to the table? In cash or kind, resources, skill sets, time, ideas or money, etc. Must be merit based!)

| |
| |
| |
| |

IREDAFENEVESHO OWOLABI

2. Who else do you need to include in the team or partner with to bring your visions into reality?

SECTION X

IREDAFENEVESHO OWOLABI

REINVENT

- **This involves reviewing and refining your methods, processes and systems such that you can produce better results with your solutions or creations.**

1. What are the traditional or conventional practices in your field that seem to be a barrier to the fulfillment of your ideas?

2. Are you willing to make a difference and disrupt the pattern of tradition? If yes, what are the new styles, methods or patterns you intend to introduce?

IREDAFENEVESHO OWOLABI

SECTION XI

IREDAFENEVESHO OWOLABI

EXPAND

- **Reaching new vistas and breaking new grounds, especially unexploited areas.**

1. Have you saturated your current market with your products and services yet?

_____

_____

_____

_____

_____

_____

_____

_____

_____

2. What plans do you have to reach new markets?

3. Are there other niches that can benefit from your product or services if you tweak them or adjust them a bit?

4. What adjustments are required?

5. What is holding you back from making those adjustments right away?

6. What have you done about this and what are you willing to do about these hindrances?

SECTION XII

AUTOMATE

- **To automate means to create systems around the idea which you have produced in a way that it can be accessed easily and quickly without your physical presence. That is the way to get alerts even when you are sleeping at night or when on vacation. This is the key to making your business work for you instead of getting caged by your produced idea or business. The internet is one of the most powerful automating machines you can use to put your business on autopilot. It has revolutionized the way we do business today. You can now become a CEO without renting a shop via the internet.**

1. How well have you automated your processes for sweat-less and effortless yields? Describe it!

2. What automated processes do you have in mind with which your executed idea can reach more people at different places at the same time?

3. What distribution channels are you currently using?

4. What other distribution channels are available to you?

5. Which ones are readily at your disposal?

SECTION XIII

IREDAFENEVESHO OWOLABI

YOUR TRADEMARK

- **A trademark represents the slogan, brand, brand promise, symbols, phrases, colours, and so on, that identifies you and makes you stand out among a pool of others. It differentiates your idea from that of others. Sensitive aspects of your productions can be stolen if not protected. Some cannot be avoided, but some can and must be guarded against.**

1. Are your creations prone to intellectual property theft or idea theft?

_____

_____

_____

2. What methods do you have in place to protect your brainchild from intellectual property crimes?

3. Have you copyrighted, trademarked or patented your idea or intellectual properties?

_____

_____

_____

_____

_____

4. Have you registered your company name or brand name? If no, when can you get one? Have you made enquires on how to get a logo for your product?

5. Do you have a logo? If No, when can you get one? If yes, have you patented your logo?

_____

_____

_____

_____

_____

SECTION XIV

IREDAFENEVESHO OWOLABI

YOUR INTERACTIONS

- **No man is an island, you will always find people around you who you can learn from through interaction.**

1. Identify the top 3 people in your field and write their names below.

_____

_____

_____

_____

_____

_____

_____

_____

2. Have you ever walked up to them or reached out to ask them the secrets to their success?

_____

_____

_____

_____

_____

If no, please reach out to them now! Appreciate their work and steer a conversation toward a direction that would bring about positive interaction with the leaders in your industry or in other related industries.

SECTION XV

YOUR OPTIMIZATIONS

- **This means to design and operate a system in a way that makes it as good as possible despite certain present moment challenges.**

1. Are you satisfied with your current results in your industry, business or career? Why?

| |
| |
| |

2. What can you do differently with your immediate resources to get more sales?

| |
| |
| |
| |
| |
| |

| |
| |
| |
| |

3. What should you stop doing now in order to optimize your production?

| |
| |
| |
| |
| |

IREDAFENEVESHO OWOLABI

SECTION XVI

SELL

- **If you do not make sales, no matter how profitable your idea is, you would never experience complete rest and satisfaction because there are bills to be paid. The fact remains however, that people must buy into you before they buy into your ideas.**

1. How best can you sell yourself? Sell yourself in these blank spaces. Feel free to go wide! Just make sure you sell yourself in a way that you would buy you!

2. Who are the people who would appreciate the ideas and creations that you have to sell?

3. Where do these people gather or where can you find them if they do not gather?

4. What irresistible offers do you have for them?

5. What are you charging for your products and/or services?

6. Why should anyone part with that money? What do they stand to get in return? Justify the price below! Make sure the value you are give is amplified above the price no matter how much it is. Play the value game here, not the price game. Weigh the gain they stand to receive when they get your product against the pain they would have to endure or suffer for not getting it.

IREDAFENEVESHO OWOLABI

PLEDGE/COMMITMENT

I _____ PLEDGE

TO TAKE ACTION IN ORDER TO DELIVER AND

TO RELEASE THE BRAINCHILD/IDEA I AM

PREGNANT WITH FOR THE BENEFIT OF THOSE

WHO I WAS ORDAINED TO HELP LIVE A

BETTER LIFE.

Signed _____

Date _____

Additional Notes

....

....

....

....

....

....

....

....

....

....

....

....

....

....

....

....

....

....

....

....

ABOUT THE AUTHOR

Iredafenevesho Owolabi (Iredafe or Dafe for short) is a Creativity Coach with the goal of helping individuals and organizations move from idea to profitable creations. He redefines public speaking with cutting-edge kingdom insights. He is happily married to the love of his life.

His books are being read in different parts of the world with countless testimonials of their impact. He mentors several aspiring authors to success via coaching calls and his book titled "How to Make Millions as An Author-preneur" is a must-have for all authors and aspiring author-preneurs who intend to master the business of their writing gift.

He speaks to different professionals and seminars via his seminars focusing on topics like Authorpreneurship, Creativity Accelerator, 4-D Thinking, Unlocking Potential, Reinvention, Kingdom etc.

To invite him or schedule him for a presentation, send him a mail via iredafeowolabi@gmail.com.

For tips and information on how to publish and market your books successfully and effectively, get "How to Make Millions as An Authorpreneur" and other books by Iredafenevesho Owolabi.

His Books include:

• Kingdom Verities

- How to Enjoy Kingdom Currency (Vol. 1)
- How to Maximize Kingdom Currency (Vol. 2)
- Kingdom Currency for Students, Graduates and Businessmen (Vol. 3)
- Kingdom Money
- Unlocking Your Kingdom Creativity
- 4-D THINKING
- Why you should Write a Book
- How to Turn your Knowledge to Money
- How to Turn Wisdom Currency to Money'
- How to Make Millions as an Author-preneur
- 18 Steps to Writing a Book Successfully
- How to Launch, Sell and Market your Books Profitably
- How To Self-Publish Your Books
- Creativity Accelerator

And lots more.

They are all available on Amazon in different formats.

www.ingramcontent.com/pod-product-compliance
Lightning Source LLC
Chambersburg PA
CBHW030714220526
45463CB00005B/2036